Kobe Bryant

─ ─ ─ ─ ─ ❧❦❧❦❧ ─ ─ ─ ─ ─

The incredible story of Kobe Bryant —
of basketball's greatest players!

Table of Contents

Introduction

Thank you for taking the time to pick up this book about Kobe Bryant!

This book serves as a biography of Kobe Bryant, one of the greatest basketball players to ever lace them up. Kobe has one of the longest, and most decorated careers of any basketball player in history, and this book aims to educate you all about it!

Throughout the following chapters, you will learn about Bryant's younger years, his journey to the NBA, his many accomplishments and records, the challenges he faced, and also what's next for the NBA champion now that he has retired from basketball.

Kobe Bryant is an incredibly inspiring athlete that everyone can learn a lot from. Both on and off the court, he strives for excellence - and usually achieves it! As you'll soon discover through reading this book, there's a lot of great life lessons we can take from the 5-time NBA champion that apply to all areas of life, not just basketball.

Once again, thanks for choosing this book, I hope you find it to be informative and entertaining!

Chapter One:

The Beginning

Kobe Bryant is, arguably, one of the most successful basketball players of our current generation. His father, a retired professional basketball player, was the inspiration behind him wanting to play. He started playing when he was just a child, and went on to be an incredible success on his high school team. He led his school to victory after victory after having several years of dry spells with the team. After finishing high school, Bryant decided to pursue a career in basketball instead of continuing his studies into college. He is one of few players who had the honor of being drafted into the NBA right out of high school. He was eventually invited to join the team that he had considered a favorite of his for quite some time, and has never once looked back.

His performance improved with every game he played, and the awards rained down upon him because of it. He has experienced many trials and tribulations during his career, such as injuries, surgeries, and sexual assault allegations, but he always addressed them head-on and found resolution to them. He is responsible for setting many new records and breaking many old ones, and he has become a household name when it comes to professional basketball.

Chapter One: The Beginning

Kobe Bryant (named after a steakhouse, believe it or not) was born in Philadelphia, Pennsylvania to NBA player Joe Bryant and Pamela Cox Bryant on August 23rd, 1978. He is the youngest sibling of three, with two older sisters, Shaya and Sharia. He grew up around the Philadelphia area and played basketball as well as soccer from a young age. Even before he came to play for the LA Lakers, he was a fan of them as well as the AC Milan soccer team. But, growing up in Pennsylvania didn't last long. At six years of age, his family moved to Rieti, Italy, so that his father could continue playing professional basketball.

However, the move is a wonderful showcase of Kobe's abilities to adapt to his surroundings and scenarios thrown at him, because he adjusted well and even learned how to speak fluent Italian. He spent the rest of his younger years there with his family, but never neglected to travel back to the States to play in a basketball summer league that he adored. Then, in 1991 his family moved back to Philadelphia after Joe Bryant's retirement from the sport. This is when Kobe was enrolled at his high school, Lower Merion, and would go on to be the saving grace that the basketball team had long been searching for.

His participation, and everything he brought to the team with his passion and skills, would drive them to win a state championship for the first time in fifty-three long years!

Kobe's middle name, Bean, comes from his father's nickname back when his father played basketball. "Jellybean" was a name that stuck with his father throughout his father's career, and the trophy name was passed down to him when Kobe was born. Bryant was raised Roman Catholic, and began learning the basics of basketball when he was only 3 years old. When Bryant's family moved to Italy, his grandfather would send him videos of NBA basketball games that Bryant constantly studied. He would analyze the different moves his favorite players made, and set about mastering them himself.

Bryant earned national recognition during a beautiful high school career. It was very rare for incoming freshman to play on varsity teams, but he earned that right with his skills right from the beginning. He was granted the option to play for the varsity team, and that put him in a position to become the first freshman in decades to start on the varsity team for his high school. However, his first year the team finished with a record of only 4–20. However, the following three years were filled with many accomplishments and turnarounds, with the Aces compiling a 77–13 record. Bryant was showing his skills and knowledge of the game by playing all five positions at various points during the games, and it earned the respect of his coach and his teammates.

During his junior year of high school, he averaged 31 points, 10 rebounds, and 5 assists, and ended up being named the Pennsylvania Player of the Year. His high level of performance continued into his senior year, where he would eventually lead his high school basketball team to a state championship. It was this title, along with the rumors of his incredible skill, that attracted the attention of college recruiters. Duke, Michigan, North Carolina, and Villanova were all at the top of the list that were vying for Bryant's attention, which is a massive accomplishment, but Bryant was nowhere near interested in college. Bryant saw Kevin Garnett picked up in the first round of the 1995 NBA draft, and that set the wheels in motion for Bryant ultimately deciding to go directly to the pros. After all, he had just seen a high school kid drafted into the big leagues without ever touching college, and it gave Bryant the confidence that he could do it as well.

At the Adidas ABCD camp, which was the camp Kobe always came back to during his summers after his family moved to Italy, Bryant earned the 1995 senior MVP award. He did all of this while playing beside Lamar Odom, who would eventually become a teammate of his within the NBA. In high school, the then-76ers coach, John Lucas, invited Bryant to workout and scrimmage with his team, and this was where he had the opportunity to play one-on-one with Jerry Stackhouse. In his senior year, Bryant led his basketball team to their first state championship. Bryant, showered with awards and attention at this point already, ended his incredible high school career as Southeastern Pennsylvania's all-time leading scorer. He had 2,883 points, which ended up surpassing both Wilt Chamberlain and Lionel Simmons, who had similar records in the area.

Apparently, he was born to break records.

Bryant won and obtained several other awards for his performance his senior year as well, including being named the Naismith High School Player of the Year, Gatorade's National Basketball Player of the Year, McDonald's All-American, and he even obtained a *USA Today* All-USA First Team Player away. Bryant's coach, Gregg Downer, made mention that he was someone who wholly and completely dominated on and off the court, and he repeatedly praised his work ethic. However, the success of his high school basketball career is what ultimately drove 17-year-old Bryant to the decision to attempt jumping directly into the NBA. The news of this venture was met with a lot of publicity, seeing as how rare the occasion was at the time. The draft of Kevin Garnett was the first pro-jump from high school that had happened in 20 solid years, and many people didn't believe that Bryant was going to be able to make it. His basketball skills and SAT score of 1080 would have ensured admission to any college of his choosing, but he was so dead-set in his decision that he didn't even visit any college campuses.

Many people rooted for him to go to college and take the safe route, but in 1996, Bryant was drafted to the Charlotte Hornets, and then quickly traded to his favorite team, the LA Lakers, at the ripe age of 17. He became, at that very moment, the youngest person to ever play for an NBA team. He was just 18 years and 72 days old when he played his first game for the Lakers. This was the first record he set upon entering the NBA, and it was an incredible foreshadowing to the records he would set, and break, throughout his entire career.

Chapter Two:

Accomplishments & Awards

Kobe Bryant is also, arguably, one of the most decorated basketball players of the current generation. He has multiple honors, awards, and records underneath his belt. He pushed himself to lengths that no regular person pushes themselves throughout his career, and it paid off in the end.

In 1996 he was drafted by the Charlotte Hornets with the 13th overall pick. However, during pre-draft workouts, Bryant made quite an impression on the then-Lakers general manager, Jerry West. West had immediately foreseen potential for Bryant on the LA Lakers. West even went as far as to officially state that Bryant's workouts were some of the best he had seen. Right after the draft, however, it was stated that the Hornets didn't have a need for Bryant, and West jumped right onto the opportunity. Fifteen days later, West traded his starting center, Vlade Divac, to the Hornets in exchange for the young Kobe Bryant.

Talk about a bad move on the Hornet's part!

Now, as a newbie, Bryant quickly earned himself a reputation as a high-flyer and a favorite of the fans by winning the 1997 Slam Dunk Contest. But not only did he win, he also broke the record for the youngest player to ever hold it. While he was only playing minutes at a time within games to begin with, he began earning more game time thanks to his rapid improvement on the court, and by the end of his first season he was averaging 15 minutes per game. He was named an All-Star by his second season, and that helped him to gain even more time out on the court because it was a physical metaphor of his capabilities within the sport. But, that was only the beginning of this career.

Bryant debuted in the Summer Pro League in Long Beach, California. He scored 25 points in front of a standing-room-only crowd, and people cheered him on in awe as seasoned defenders struggled to get in front of him. After already being drafted to the Hornets, and then being traded to the Lakers, West and Del Harris (another Lakers coach) were absolutely thrilled with his performance. In that particular competition, he ended up scoring 36 points in the finale alone, and finished with an average of 24 points and 5 rebounds within the four games.

In 1999, he ended up becoming part of the All-NBA, All-Defensive, and All-Star teams, further proving his understanding and skill of and within the sport, and this ended up being the turning point for him. People stopped seeing him as a little boy on the court and began seeing a professional player blossoming alongside his team. Later on, even though there was a feud between the two, Bryant and Shaquille O'Neal would eventually lead the Lakers to three consecutive championships from 2000 to 2002.

In his second season, he obtained more playing time and began to show even more of his abilities as a talented young basketball player. Because of this uptick in time on the court, Bryant's point averages more than doubled. He went from 7 points a game to 15 points a game, and with that uptick in numbers would, of course, come even more court time. Bryant was the runner-up for the NBA's Man of the Year Award, and, through fan voting, he ended up becoming the youngest NBA All-Star starter in its history! He was eventually joined by teammates O'Neal, Van Exel, and Jones, which made it the first time since 1983 that four players on the same team were chosen to play in the same All-Star Game. And, of course, because of Bryant's impressive numbers and scores throughout any one game, his average of 15 points per game ended up being the highest of any non-starter in the season.

Bryant was made to break records.

The 1998–99 season would mark Bryant's emergence as one of the top guards in the league. Bryant started every game, and it was during this season that Bryant signed a 6-year contract extension worth $70 million. This contract kept him with the Lakers until the end of the 2003–04 season. However, in the 2000-2001 season, Bryant's outstanding contributions to the game, and to his team, helped them win their second consecutive championship title. In the 2001-02 season, he played a whopping 80 games and averaged 25 points per game, as well as helped his team complete a hat-trick. Then, another record came along: he was the youngest player, at only 23 years of age, to win three NBA titles.

Once O'Neal was traded to the Miami Heat after the 2003–04 season, Bryant ended up becoming the cornerstone of the Lakers franchise. He would lead the NBA in scoring during the 2005–06 and 2006–07 seasons, and, in 2006, Bryant would end up scoring a career-high 81 points against the Toronto Raptors. And, you guessed it, it was another record set. That game with those points would end up being the second-highest number of points scored in a game in NBA history, second only to Wilt Chamberlain's 100-point performance in a single game.

Then, for the 2007-08 season, Bryant was awarded the regular season's MVP Award as well as lead his team to the 2008 NBA Finals as the first seed in the Western Conference. Pretty soon, Bryant saw his potential for the Olympics, and was given the opportunity to play in the 2008 Summer Olympics in Beijing. He won a gold medal as a member of the U.S. men's basketball team, and brought that gold proudly home to a country that was cheering him on every step of the way. In his career, he led the Lakers to two more championships in 2009 and 2010, and he took the MVP Award home for both championship series.

Bryant currently ranks third on the league's all-time post-season scoring list as well as the all-time regular season scoring list. He has been selected for 15 All-NBA Teams opportunities as well as 12 All-Defensive Team opportunities. He was selected to play in the NBA All-Star Game on 18 separate occasions, and many of those occasions brought him the opportunity to win the All Star MVP award. He won this award in: 2002, 2007, 2009 (which he shared with O'Neal) and 2011.

The awards and recognitions that Kobe Bryant has been bestowed with are numerous and long-winded. Multiple awards have been won multiple times, and many records have been shattered by him. Whether it was his father's influence as a young boy or his own passion for the game that flourished at such a young age, it is very obvious that not only was he talented, he was also competent when it came to the strategies of the game. Bryant is a 5-time NBA champion, a 2-time NBA finals MVP, a 2-time scoring champion, an NBA All-Rookie Team selection, and a 17-time player of the month. He racked up multiple recognitions given within a regular NBA season, from most points per game all the way to usage percentage. He is a 2-time Best NBA Player ESPY Award winner, as well as an overall NBA playoffs leader. If there is ever a basketball player to look up to in terms of skill, overall achievement within the sport, and knowledge of the court's strategies, Bryant has all of the requirements necessary to meet your needs.

Not only that, but Bryant holds a slew of records, both new to the industry as well as ones that shattered previous records. He holds the record for the most seasons played for one single NBA franchise, most field goal attempts, most points scored in one arena, most games played at one arena, and the youngest player to ever score 33,000 points in the lifetime of his career. And, however impressive those might be, there are records that he set that were never in play, and have never been surpassed since he set them. Some of these include being the only player in NBA history with more than 30,000 points, 6,000 assists and 6,000 rebounds underneath his lifetime career belt, as well as being the only player in the history of the NBA to score at least 600 points in the postseason for three consecutive years.

Kobe Bryant is a force to be reckoned with in the basketball world. It takes a very specific combination of genetics, determination, and commitment to be able to achieve the types of things that he has throughout his career. Bryant's career is riddled with prestige, hard work, and physical trophies for that hard work. It's very easy to understand why he is being considered for the Naismith Memorial Basketball Hall of Fame in 2021.

Chapter Three:

Winning Championships

Bryant continued to succeed in his career. The hard work and dedication that he put into his craft was made obvious by his overt success in the sport. From learning the basics as a toddler with his father all the way to leading his high school team to a championship after 53 years is only the beginning of a testament to his skills and prowess. Bryant changed the face of the game when he was drafted right out of high school, and quickly began breaking records, as well as setting new ones, right from the beginning. And, as if his fortune couldn't be any better, the tides would shift dramatically, yet again, as soon as Phil Jackson became the coach for the Lakers in 1999.

After years of consistent and steady improvement in his game and his skills, Bryant was now one of the top shooting guards in the league. This title is what earned him appearances in the league's All-NBA, All-Star, and All-Defensive teams. Bryant and O'Neal formed a record-setting center-guard combination, and the Lakers soon found themselves as championship contenders. Jackson ended up using the legendary triangle offense he used to win six championships with the Chicago Bulls, and this is what helped both Bryant and O'Neal rise to be considered some of the elite in the NBA. After this evolution and rebranding, there were three consecutive championships (2000, 2001, and 2002) won with this technique and talent-driven team.

However, every story has a rise and fall, and it was only so long before Kobe hit his first downfall. Bryant started the 1999–00 season on the sidelines for six weeks due to an injury to his hand. He obtained it during a preseason game against the Washington Wizards, and the team struggled without him on the court. However, Bryant soon got back to playing over 38 minutes per game, and the Lakers saw their statistics and scores begin to rise whenever he marched back onto that court for the season. Not only that, but Bryant ended up leading the team in assists *and* steals per game. Talk about a comeback!

The duo of the season, O'Neal and Bryant, along with the backing of a strong bench led to the outcome of the Lakers winning 67 games. That total tied for fifth-most in NBA history. Bryant was named to the All-NBA Team Second Team and All-NBA Defensive Team for the first time in his career, and it made him the youngest player to receive defensive honors. But, tragedy struck his body again on the courts. In the 2000 Finals against the Indiana Pacers, Bryant ended up injuring his ankle after landing on Jalen Rose's foot.

But, in a nasty turn of events, Rose later admitted he placed his foot under Bryant intentionally with the purpose of tripping him up. Bryant did not return to that game, and he also missed Game 3 due to the injury as well. However, in Game 4 Bryant scored 22 points in the second half (despite his injury) and led the team to an overtime victory. Bryant scored the winning shot, brought the Lakers to championship victory, and all despite of the injury to his ankle that put him out of Game 2. That type of feat doesn't just take practice and determination, it takes confidence and love for the game to play through something like that, and that is exactly that Bryant had.

Statistically, the 2000–01 season saw Bryant perform similarly to his previous year, but his average points per game went up. However, no good story is ever without rivalry, and this was also the year when disagreements between Bryant and O'Neal began to surface in the media. Bryant still led the team in assists with 5 per game, but the Lakers didn't win as many games this particular season. But, they still made it to the playoffs, and brought home their second championship despite a loss during the playoffs that dropped them in rank. During the playoffs, Bryant played as much as he possibly could, which brought his stats up to 29 points, 7 rebounds, and 6 assists per game. And that was with all of the injuries he had sustained!

In the 2001–02 season, Bryant played 80 games for the first time in his career. He claimed his first All-Star MVP trophy during this season after a 31-point performance in Philadelphia, but he was loudly booed by fans, dampening the occasion. These boos that happened all throughout the game, and all throughout his trophy ceremony, stemmed from an earlier comment he had made to a heckler from the 76ers. However, he didn't let any of that deter him from what he knew he deserved with the performances he had given over his budding career. He made the All-NBA Defensive team again, but he was also promoted to the All-NBA First Team for the first time in his career, which was a massive accomplishment for Bryant. But, amidst all of this good, negative things still lingered. However, this time it was Bryant's fault. Kobe was suspended for one game after he punched Reggie Miller of the Indiana Pacers, after a Lakers' victory.

The Lakers would continue though, and eventually win a championship over the Sacramento Kings despite not having the home-court advantage. They played all seven games, which is something that had not happened to them since the 2000 Western Conference Finals, but the Lakers got the job done in the end. With this win, it brought Bryant yet another record to add to his belt: at the young age of 23, Bryant had become the youngest player to win three championships. Throughout all of this, and all of the prestige and the competency for his sport that he displayed throughout this particular battle for a championship, all of his accomplishments, statistics, and athletic prowess cemented Bryant's reputation as a clutch player and a necessary component of his NBA team.

The work that Bryant put into honing his skills from such a young age is what brought him to be athlete that he was during his career. The skills his father implanted into him when he was younger, the camps that he traveled back to the States for in order to perfect his skills, the tapes that his grandparents would send overseas for him to analyze, and even the team he played with in high school all culminated into the 17-year old that was drafted out of high school to the pros. His confidence for the game can be seen in his ability to keep his composure on court, despite efforts from other teams attempting to hurt him, or aggravate him, in order to get him ejected from games. That type of leadership and confidence, as well as a sense of self, can only come from the years of hard work and training that groomed Kobe to have the confidence in himself that he had. Being traded to his favorite team just 15 days into his initial draft only brought about more respect for the game because he was playing for a people, and a city, that he loved and respected.

But, every great leader, athlete, and world-influencer has their downfalls, and Kobe Bryant would hit his when accusations of sexual assault would rise up from Colorado, forever tainting him in the eyes of many of his fans. His career was riddled with records and promising statistics and history-setting plays, but it also boasted of a darker side that Kobe attempted to settle in the privacy of his own life.

Chapter Four:

Challenges

No career like Kobe Bryant's is going to be squeaky clean. Things will always come into the spotlight that are negative in connotation, and also in reality. In 2003, Bryant was accused of sexual assault in the state of Colorado. The media reported that Kobe had been arrested in connection with an investigation that was pending because of complaints and accusations filed by a 19-year old employee of the hotel where he was staying. He was there for a scheduled surgery, and the young woman accused him of raping her in his room the night before he was scheduled to go under the knife. Bryant openly admitted to the sexual encounter that occurred, but denied the fact that is was forced. He kept insisting that the encounter was consensual on both ends, and the case was eventually dropped when the young woman that accused him refused to testify in court. However, a civil case was filed shortly thereafter, and was settled out of court. The agreement, along with a monetary settlement, included him publicly apologizing, even though he never admitted guilt.

After the allegations, many of Bryant's endorsers (such as Nike and Coca-Cola) dropped out of supporting him. His season was forever tainted, and people speculate that the reason he did so poorly that year was because of all of the attention and media presence surrounding the incident. It is, to date, one of Bryant's worst seasons on record. To make matters worse, around eight months after the incident, the Lodge & Spa at Cordillera (the hotel that Bryant had been staying at for his surgery) remodeled a part of their hotel and ended up selling off some furniture. It was highly speculated that the remodeling was the area of Bryant's room, and that some of the furniture sold off was from Room 35, where the incident had taken place. The lodge denied any claims to the validity of those media-speculated statements, but it didn't stop the press from repeatedly drilling it into the public's minds.

Bryant was closely watched, scrutinized, and criticized during the 2004–05 season. His reputation had been badly damaged from everything that had happened during the previous year, and the blows just kept on coming. A particularly damaging shot was fired when Phil Jackson, the Laker's coach, wrote *The Last Season: A Team in Search of Its Soul*. The book described in great detail the events of the Lakers' tumultuous 2003–04 season and had a number of criticisms of Bryant. In the book, Jackson called Bryant un-coachable, and even went so far as to criticize his behind-the-scenes antics with his teammates. The book was just another blow dealt in a series of endless hits that Bryant was having trouble recuperating from.

There were other blows that Bryant took throughout his career that poorly reflected him in the eyes of his fans and the media. During the 2006-07 season, Bryant got himself involved in many other on-court incidents. In one game, he had attempted to draw contact on a game-winning shot that the opposing team was attempting to make, and he flailed his arm. He ended up striking San Antonio Spurs guard Manu Ginobili in the face, and a league review quickly followed. Bryant was suspended at the conclusion of the review, taking him out of a Madison Square Garden game against the Knicks. They came to the conclusion that Bryant had made an unnatural movement in swinging his arm backwards, and, therefore, it was ruled intentional. But, apparently Bryant didn't learn from this first lesson, because he would repeat the motion in a game with the Minnesota Timberwolves, striking guard Marko Jaric. It was after this second incident that the NBA would hand Bryant his second one-game suspension.

Then, in April of 2011, Kobe Bryant was fined $100,000 for directing an anti-gay slur at a referee out of frustration. The Gay & Lesbian Alliance Against Defamation ended up getting involved, and eventually praised the NBA's overall decision to fine Bryant. The Human Rights Campaign came out in the media and condemned Bryant's language as disgraceful and distasteful, as well as intolerant. Kobe then made a public statement saying that he was open to discussing the matter with multiple gay rights groups, and ended up appealing his fine. Later on, he apologized fully for using the slur that he did. But, with this outpouring of tension against Bryant came the opposition of his teammates, who appeared in a Lakers public service announcement to state that Bryant's slurs were not a reflection of the team's opinions and beliefs as a whole. They denounced his behavior, and it further tainted Bryant's reputation in the eyes of his fans and the public.

But, as always, things started to look up for Bryant again about a year later when he signed a $136-million contract. He regained some of his endorsements, like Coca-Cola, Nike, and Spalding, and even went on to be named the NBA's Most Valuable Player in 2008. But, things didn't stay as nice as he would have liked, because in 2011, Bryant's wife filed for divorce citing irreconcilable differences. The emotional struggle was, once again, seen on the court, and his teammates became increasingly worried about him throughout the seasons. Through it all, however, Bryant was able to patch things up with his wife, and the divorce was dropped in January of 2013.

Through it all, no matter your opinion of Bryant, he continued to be the absolute best he could be under the circumstances. After the Lakers ended up losing the 2004 NBA Finals, O'Neal was traded to the Miami Heat, which meant that Bryant would become the major influencer and player for the Lakers. He led the NBA in scoring during the 2005–06 and 2006–07 seasons, showing that, despite the negative media coverage and the retreat by some of his fans, that he was still the same skilled athlete that he had always been.

Bryant was awarded the regular season's MVP Award in 2008, and continued to be among the top players in the league through 'til 2013. However, the buck stops there again when Bryant, now 34 years old, tore his Achilles tendon. He recovered, but his play on the court was limited because he ended up sustaining even more injuries. He acquired season-ending injuries to his shoulder and his knee, which would mark the slow decline of Bryant's professional career. Never fully recuperating, Bryant would cite his physical decline as the reason that that he would be retiring after the 2015–16 season when he made the personal decision public.

Throughout the entirety of Kobe Bryant's career, rumors had always surfaced that him and Shaquille O'Neal had a private feud with each other. This was a media-created rivalry that spun off and circulated through the fans for years. They played wonderfully on the court together, and were even cited as the dream duo to have for any team looking to win long-term championships. But, that didn't stop the media from scrutinizing and picking random events apart, creating this smokescreen of a feud that followed both O'Neal and Bryant throughout their entire careers. Apparently, when Bryant first joined the Lakers, it was said that O'Neal stated that he wouldn't be babysitting, implying that Bryant would never be able to live up to the expectations of playing professionally because of his age and the attitude that usually comes with it. Bryant's confidence at such a young age on the court was interpreted as arrogance, and thus was born a feud that never seriously existed.

While O'Neal is said to have given Bryant a hard time during his first couple of seasons, there were many things that were misinterpreted on both sides that stuck with the both of them throughout their careers. Bryant's professionalism and unwillingness to verbally spar in a humorous manner in interviews with his teammates was misinterpreted as selfishness, and O'Neal was even accused of hazing Bryant his first season on the team. While those accusations were never proven, it was when O'Neal comforted Bryant after a bad game performance that people began to wonder if they had made amends and started a new journey together.

However, the rough waters that dotted his career also stand beside some of the best accomplishments of any basketball player that had come before him, and the most notable moments in his career completely overshadowed the down times that he experienced.

Chapter Five:

More Records

E ven with the pitfalls and the media coverage that ensued from it, Bryant played his entire 20-year career with the Los Angeles Lakers, and ended up winning five NBA championships with them. As we've discussed, his career is full to the brim with awards, recognitions, tributes, and trophies.

But between winning championships and receiving MVP awards, Kobe set even more astonishing records. Bryant became the youngest player in NBA history to reach 30,000 career points...and he was only 34. He also found himself becoming the all-time leading scorer in Lakers franchise history in 2010 after surpassing Jerry West.

After his second year with the NBA, Bryant was chosen to start on every All-Star Game until his retirement. The 18 consecutive appearances mounted for yet another record that he would maintain, and within those appearances he won four All-Star MVP Awards, which tied him for the most in NBA history. But those accomplishments didn't stop pouring in. At the Summer Olympics of 2008 and 2012, he brought home gold medals for playing on the U.S. national team. *Sporting News* and TNT even named Bryant the top NBA player of the 2000s!

On January 22, 2006, the record that would define his career happened. He scored a career-high 81 points in a 122–104 victory against the Toronto Raptors, earning him a spot as the second-highest point earner in any given game in NBA history. The title was originally held by Elgin Baylor with a 71-point game, and was only surpassed by Chamberlain's 100-point game in 1962. However, many people understood the difference between Chamberlain's 100-point game and Bryant's 81-point game, and there are many people that believe that, even though Bryant holds the second highest ranking title, that his game proves much more skill behind his accomplishment.

It is said that Chamberlain was fed the ball repeatedly by teammates for inside shots in their blowout win, but if you watch Bryant's game, it is very clear that he created his own shots from the outside. In that particular game, the Lakers trailed at halftime by 14 and didn't actually pull ahead until the fourth quarter. The comeback was thanks to Bryant's ability to create his own shot. There are many people who also look at the percentages: Chamberlain's pointed accounted for 59% of his team's overall score in Philadelphia's 169–147 win, which is lower than Bryant's 66% of the Lakers' 122 points in their game with the Raptors.

This particular year was massive for Bryant, because in that same month, he also became the first player since 1964 to score at least 45 points in four consecutive games. That title wasn't superseded, but merely joined him alongside Chamberlain and Baylor as the only players ever to achieve this feat. But the records that he was making and breaking weren't just for him, they were also reflecting back onto his team. By the end of the 2005–06 season, Bryant set single-season franchise records for his team for the most 40-point games played (with a whopping 27 games that had him scoring

40 or more points) and most points scored throughout the season (a massive 2,832 points tallied by the end of the season). He also won the league's scoring title for the first time that season, which made him only the fifth player in NBA history to average at least 35 points every game in one season.

However, there is also another feat that he accomplished during this same season, and that was to score three back to back 50-plus point games in a row. This was something that had only been done by two people before him: Michael Jordan, who accomplished it in 1987; and Baylor, in 1962. Bryant finished that season with ten total 50-plus point games, matching Chamberlain's performance during one of his seasons. In this 2006-07 season, where all of these skilled accomplishments were taking place, his jersey became the highest-selling jersey in China and the U.S.

Kobe Bryant has a massive list of accomplishments, records and achievements underneath his name. Minus the ones already mentioned, he is still, arguably, one of the most decorated basketball players to ever grace the courts. His hard work and dedication to the game paid off in many areas most people don't even realize, and it was those small and insignificant accomplishments that led him to bloom into the fierce competitor and legendary player that we remember him as. Bryant was competitive, dedicated, professional within the realms of his basketball career, and even though it alienated some of his teammates, it led to one of the longest lists of accomplishments that any one basketball player can boast of.

Below is a comprehensive list of his recognitions and achievements:

Currently held records

- Most Seasons played for a single NBA Franchise

- Most All-Star Game MVP awards won over the course of their career (tied with Bob Pettit)

- Most All-Star Game field goals made for their career

- Most offensive rebounds in an All-Star Game

- Most All-NBA Total Selections won for their career (tied with Kareem Abdul Jabbar and Tim Duncan)

- Most All-NBA First Team honors won over their career (tied with Karl Malone)

- Most All-Defensive First Team honors won over their career (tied with Michael Jordan, Gary Payton, and Kevin Garnett)

- Only player in NBA history with more than 30,000 points, 6,000 assists and 6,000 rebounds.

- Most three-point field goal attempts for career-playoffs

- Most field goal attempts for career-playoffs

- Most three-point field goal attempts for career-finals

- Most free throws made in four-game playoff series (second round vs. Sacramento Kings in 2001)

- Most points scored in one arena over their career: 16,161 (as of April 14, 2016, at Staples Center, Los Angeles)

- Most games played at one arena over their career: 599 (as of April 14, 2016, at Staples Center, Los Angeles

- Highest Score against rest of teams in the league above 40 (shared with Bob Pettit)

- Youngest player to score 33,000 points in his career

- Youngest player to be named to the NBA All-Rookie Team

- Youngest player to be named to the NBA All-Defensive Team

- Youngest player to start a game

- Youngest player to win the NBA Slam Dunk Championship

- Youngest player to start an All-Star game

- Only player in NBA history to score at least 600 points in the postseason for three consecutive years. [633 (2008), 695 (2009), 671 (2010)]

- Oldest player to score 60+ points, one game

NBA Awards and Accomplishments

- 5-time NBA champion

- 2-time NBA Finals MVP Awards

Chapter Five: More Records

- NBA Most Valuable Player

- 2-time scoring champion

- 4-time NBA All-Star Game

- NBA Slam Dunk Contest champion

- 17-time Player of the Month

Lakers Franchise Records

- Most seasons played

- Most playoff seasons played

- Most All-Star Game Selections

- Most All-NBA First Team

- Most All-Defensive First Team

- Most career points

- Most career playoff points

- Most per-season points

- Highest game point total

- Most games scoring 60-plus points

- Most games scoring 50-plus points

- Most games scoring 50-plus points for the season

- Most games scoring 40-plus points

- Most games scoring 40-plus points for the season

- Most minutes played during a career

- Most minutes played during career playoffs

Chapter Six:

Work Ethic

Kobe Bryant has put in an astounding amount of work in order to become the legend that he became. From training very early on with his father all the way to using his excess time in high school to train outside of the season, Bryant has showed everyone that being the best takes a level of commitment that not everyone is ready for. His coaches have even told us in interviews that, while on the road, Kobe would wake up three hours before everyone else to get a decent workout in before sitting down with everyone for breakfast. Three hours! Bryant would wake up at 5 AM to run drills and exercise of his own volition before participating in breakfast at 8 AM with his team, before running team drills together. Even his former teammate, John Celestand, admitted that Kobe was always the first player in the gym, even if he was hurt. There was a time during the 1999-00 season where Kobe had broken his wrist, but instead of taking the time off, Kobe had shown up to the gym and was dribbling and shooting with one hand. It is stated that during the season, Bryant would practice four hours a day, and even more during the off-season!

Bryant said that it gave him an excuse to work on the accuracy of his less-dominant hand. That is a level of dedication that not everyone has.

For example, when the Summer Olympics of 2012 came around, he knew that his knees were giving out on him. So, what did he decide to do? He decided to shed 16 pounds so that he could play to the best of his ability during the Olympic Games. He ended up completely kicking pizza as well as all sugars, natural and otherwise, in order to shed the weight. Now, Bryant has never been an out of shape person. You can't possibly be with the way he trains and plays. But, he recognized his body's limits, decided that he wanted to play these games, and set out to do what he had to. It was a diet he would ultimately keep going throughout the rest of his career, stating that many athletes don't self-assess, which is necessary to play, and be, your best.

In high school, whether he was in-season or in the off-season, he would show up to practice on his own in the gymnasium at 5 AM before leaving at 7 AM to go get ready for school every single morning. There are people that reported that, unless Bryant was sick and completely out of school, he was there every single morning running drills by himself and practicing his shooting and his agility on the court. Sound familiar? But not only that, he would constantly bug his teammates to play 1-on-1 games with him all the way to 100 points. Yes, 100 points. It has been reported that, in his worst game, he still beat his teammate 100-12. He would keep this trend up throughout his professional career by keeping some of his teammates after practice as guinea pigs for new moves that he was wanting to try out on the court.

When in practice, Kobe would always count his made shots, and he wouldn't stop until he got to 400. If he didn't make it to that number in practice? Well, he would just stay after everyone was gone. O'Neal even admitted that he would catch Kobe in the gym sometimes practicing without a ball. He would be simulating plays and dribbling and practicing shots, but he wouldn't actually have a ball in his hand so that he could clock anytime he tripped up or lost focus. Yes, he is a perfectionist, and it doesn't just show in his on-the-court practice and dedication. It also shows in his endorsements. When Nike wanted to endorse Bryant, he was ecstatic. But, he had just one condition: he wanted them to shave a few millimeters off the bottoms of his shoes so that he could get a hundredth of a second's worth of better reaction time. The man was so dedicated that he even tailored his clothes so that he could perform his best.

Bryant also has a massive dedication to his body. While the giving out of his body is what ultimately led to his retirement, during all of those seasons played he would ice his knees for 20 minutes three times a day and would also have regular acupuncture sessions in order to reduce the risk of him getting hurt. Then, when he was hurt, he would still continue to show his dedication through cold-calling successful business people and entrepreneurs to ask them about their secrets to success so that he could implement them in his own life. It seems as if Bryant never stopped to take a selfish breath for himself whenever he was in professional mode! An NBA scout in 2008 stated that the reason Bryant was so successful on the court was because he loved doing all of the things that were required off of the court. And that scout is exactly right.

He never wastes any moment, in fact. During half time in all of his games, he would rally his team members around a laptop so that they could watch bits and pieces of the first half of the game. This would give them the opportunity to not only critique their own playing, but to find weaknesses within the other team's playing so that they could carve out better shots for themselves. His work ethic was so impressive, in fact, that Michael Jordan himself called it out in one of his biographies, stating that Bryant was the only person he felt whose work ethic and dedication to the game rivaled his own. Talk about a serious compliment.

But, there is no rest for the weary, even with compliments like that. On game days, his teammates admitted that those were some of the hardest workouts that Bryant would run. You would think that someone would rest on a game day in order to keep their health, and their body, in line. But not Bryant. He had drills that he would run that would help him block out all of the excess noise, focus his mind for the game, and get his blood pumping so that he could be hyped for the game ahead.

Bryant's obvious dedication to his craft, his body, and his game is what has earned him the honor of being a household name when someone talks about basketball. From the times he spent learning with his father all the way up to his very last basketball game, Bryant was running behind the scenes doing absolutely everything necessary to make sure he was always at the top of his game. Many players, like O'Neal, would fall back on their size as their main strategy in a game, but not Bryant. He made sure that his main fallback during games was his inherent love, talent, and physical prowess behind the game of basketball. He would practice with teammates and he would practice alone. He would practice with or without a ball, and he would practice early in the mornings before anyone else. He would cold-call people for advice on success when he couldn't practice, and he was in the locker room dissecting game footage whenever the team was resting during half-time.

There are also many rumors, most steeped in truth, that swirl Kobe Bryant's work ethic as well. For instance, Jamal Crawford once told a story about how he heard of Bryant practicing a shot for a solid hour. One specific shot from one specific place on an empty court for a solid hour. The kicker? It wasn't something epic like a three-pointer shot, it was a miniscule shot from a marginal distance from the net. Gary Payton remembers some of Kobe's first words to him. He says that he recalls a conversation he had on the bus when Kobe was no older than 18, and in that conversation Kobe stated that he was going to make himself the number one scorer for the Lakers and that he was going to win five or six championships. Yes, those words were actually stated by Bryant himself when his career had barely started. The point? Kobe Bryant isn't incredible by design or chance. He is incredible because he works the hardest of anyone else to be that way. That, in and of itself, makes his work ethic and determination stand out from the crowd.

Bryant wasn't just a success to the game, he was a success in writing the map of dedication necessary to be the best in your field, no matter what your field is. His work ethic and dedication made him a household name in basketball, but his actions on and off the court taught us how to use every single second of our time to further ourselves in any chosen professional field.

Chapter Seven:

What's Next for Kobe?

Kobe Bryant's last official game was April 3rd, 2016. He played it at the STAPLES Center at 37 years of age, and an estimated 5.2 million people tuned in to watch. He scored 60 total points that game in front of a packed stadium of over 18,000 people, and when he walked off of the court, people stood to their feet and chanted his name. His legacy will live on, and you can rest assured that you will see his name in the Hall of Fame pretty soon.

But, what comes next? For a young man like Bryant, much of his life is still ahead of him. Many believed that he would grieve the loss of the NBA, but that is actually not the case. Bryant has stated that there is a balance to the world, life, and death. There are beginnings and endings to everything in life, and he understood coming in that, one day, his career would have to end. In that regard, he says that he felt ready for his impending retirement, and doesn't regret it one bit.

Some very deep thoughts from one of the world's more infamous NBA professionals.

One of the first things that happened early on in his retirement is that Bryant and his family announced that his wife was expecting their third child. A little girl, to be exact. He said that his family was incredibly excited for their new addition and that he was coaching his children on their newfound responsibilities once the little bundle of joy arrived. His wife, Vanessa, gave birth to their third child in December of 2016.

But what about his career? Will there ever be an NBA comeback? Well, Kobe has already answered that question, and his answer is no. He doesn't foresee a comeback to the NBA, nor does he see himself as a sports announcer, despite the many opportunities that have been presented to him to do so since his retirement. Many will actually be surprised that Kobe boasts of a creative side. He has stated that he enjoys creating and producing content, and claims that he enjoys storytelling. His self-proclaimed mythological universe that he has created in his imagination has elements that he wants to try and bring to life. However, Bryant admits that he isn't the best out there for bringing his stories to life. He has compared himself to Walt Disney, stating that Walt did well with animation, but understood that there were people that were better. So, he employed those people and collaborated with them, and eventually built the empire that Disney is today.

Talk about lofty goals! But really, do we even doubt it, given all that he has accomplished in the NBA?

He jokingly tells people that he's trying not to gain 100 points. But, there is some truth to that statement. Despite Bryant's numerous surgeries and injuries, he is still keeping himself in prime physical shape. He has stated in several interviews that he stays away from the court, but he still does quite a bit of running. He hops on the treadmill and runs, he uses it to do sprints, and he even works on his interval training. Seems that he's taken those healthy habits from the NBA and applied them to his retirement!

With Bryant's influence on the shoe and sneaker industry, it isn't a shocker that they gave him his own signature shoe line. But, that isn't all that Kobe is up to nowadays. He also has his own media and venture capitalist company.

Yes, you read that right.

With his creative side, Kobe decided to venture into the film and television industry. He claims that his obsession for creating and producing content is the same obsession that he had for basketball. He has thrown the same amount of dedication and commitment behind this venture, and understands that this is how you now influence a generation. He has recognized the power of media, and he wants to utilize it to influence future generations like he did with his basketball career. His production company, Kobe Studios, is creating inspirational stories such as Dear Basketball, where he had the opportunity to work with Glen Keane and John Williams. This animated short was put together by the three of them, and centered around Bryant's open letter to basketball about his retirement. Kobe called the project "ridiculously fun," and he has decided to keep pursuing projects with Kobe Studios.

But, that isn't all. Alongside Kobe Studios is also Bryant's venture capitalist firm. He partnered up with Jeff Stibel to fund and launch Bryant-Stibel. Stibel does the heavy-lifting, which is helping to provide guidance to the companies that they help monetarily, while Bryant handles the marketing and the storytelling. They have already invested in 15 separate companies and are contributing over $100-million of their own money into the newly-launched firm. While he launched Kobe Studios on the eve of his retirement, making it a knee-jerk venture that he had always wanted to pursue, he thought long and hard about pursuing a venture capitalist firm before coming across Stibel. It was actually Stibel's expertise, coupled with Bryant's desire to help other people like himself become successful in their arena, that led to the creation of this firm. Many people scoff at him and tell him to "stay in his lane" when it comes to business versus basketball, but Bryant is determined to take these two ventures by the horns.

But, even with what people whisper behind his back, Bryant seems to always make time for his team and the people that helped him achieve victory after victory within his career. It's almost as if his day has more hours in it than everyone else! His teammates state that he comes around, and Kobe boasts that he watches every single Lakers game as he cheers on his friends and his team. He gets together with his coaches every once in a while, and sometimes Kobe even shows up to practices and gets in on the action. Of course, Bryant has said that he doesn't miss it. He has stated that he enjoys kicking his feet up and watching the Lakers games, but he admits that the NBA was his entire existence for 20 years, and that you have to come off of something like that slowly. This was his life for two decades, and he knew that if he was to enjoy retirement the way he wanted to, that he had to make sure to make time in his life for something that had encompassed such a massive part of it for so long.

Admittedly, Bryant's retirement future is a little scattered. Some of his fans think he has too much money, and others think he is bored. Many are rooting for some sort of NBA comeback, and it's not shocking that they would speculate about this happening. On the one hand, he has this creative side that is aching to be released with his self-proclaimed storytelling talents; and, on the other hand, he has a venture capitalist firm that he wants to utilize in order to help young people kickstart their businesses.

Kobe Studios is a passion, but Bryant-Stibel is almost nostalgic for him. As a young man who was drafted right out of high school into a professional sports team that was given the opportunity to make a career out of something that he had passion for, it's no wonder that Kobe now wants to help young businesses and business owners do the same thing. Will he succeed? Well, if the past is any indicator of future behavior and trajectory, then we can most certainly believe that he will. After all, Kobe Bryant taught us that anything was possible if you were willing to work harder than anyone else to achieve it.

And I believe he's right.

Conclusion

Thanks again for taking the time to read this book!

You should now have a good understanding of Kobe Bryant and his inspiring life and career!

If you enjoyed this book, please take the time to leave me a review on Amazon. I appreciate your honest feedback, and it really helps me to continue producing high quality books.

CPSIA information can be obtained
at www.ICGtesting.com
Printed in the USA
LVHW081752270122
709435LV00006B/263